SHIP OF FOOL

For Morri,

brother poet and
valued friend, with
best regards,

Bill
2/20/1

SHIP OF FOOL

POEMS BY

WILLIAM TROWBRIDGE

Wm. Trowbridge

Red Hen Press | *Pasadena, CA*

Ship of Fool

Book design by Mark E. Cull

Book layout by Kathrine Davidson

Library of Congress Cataloging-in-Publication Data

Trowbridge, William, 1941 –

Ship of Fool : poems / by William Trowbridge.—1st ed.

  p. cm.

ISBN 978-1-59709-446-7

I. Title.

PS3570.R66S55 2011

811'.54—dc22

                    2010040776

Los Angeles County Arts Commission, California Arts Council, National Endowment for the Arts, and Department of Cultural Affairs partially support Red Hen Press.

First Edition

Published by Red Hen Press

Pasadena, CA

www.redhen.org

ACKNOWLEDGEMENTS

Thanks are due to the following periodicals in whose pages these poems first appeared: *Abyss & Apex*, "Alone No More" in earlier version; *Boulevard*, "Bully," "My Father's Laugh"; *The Chariton Review*, "Naked in Public"; *Crab Orchard Review*, "Pantsing Bobby Freeman in Fifth Grade," "Prodigy"; *88*, "Coach Said"; *Free Lunch*, "Foolproof"; *The Gettysburg Review*, "Fool's Paradise," "Fool and His Money," "The Consolation of Philosophy," "The Right Stuff," "Psycholinguistics," "King of Fools," "The Juggler," "Obedience," "Class of '59"; *Green Mountains Review*, "World's Biggest Fool"; *Great River Review*, "School Lesson"; *I-70 Review*, "Ship of Fool," "Fool's Wager"; *The Iowa Review*, "Fool for Love," "Fools Give You Reasons," "Pity the Fool"; *Little Balkans Review*, "That's Entertainment"; *Margie*, "Cabfare from the Airport," "Why Fool Voted No-Nonsense," "Fool Demonstrates His Invention"; *New Letters*, "The Palmer Method," "Speed," "Basic Fool," "Danse Macabre," "Flight of the Fool, 1902"; *Nebraska Review*, "Movie with the Guys"; *New Madrid*, "The Incredible Shrinking Fool," "The Fool Tree"; *Poems & Plays*, "Roll Out the Fool," "Lycanthropy"; *Revista Neo*, "Foolin' Around," "The Perfect Fool"; *Shawangunk Review*, "Alone No More," "Fool's Family Album"; *River Styx*, "The Art of Motorcycle Maintenance," "Fool Noir," "Playing the Fool"; *The Tampa Review*, "Seismic"; *Tar River Poetry*, "Dickhead," "Foolish Tears," "Ninety-seven-pound Fool," "Fool Rushes In," "Fool Expelled from Eden," "Wise Fool," "Rental Tux."

Thanks are also due to the following friends who gave welcome encouragement and criticism: Charles Harper Webb, Jeff Mock, Jim Simmerman, Catie Rosemurgy, Leigh Allison Wilson, David Slater, and John Wood.

Thanks, finally, to The Anderson Center, within whose facilities a number of these poems were written, and to its director, Robert Hedin.

For Howard Nemerov, whose poems inspired me to try
writing my own and whose encouragement kept me at it.

Contents

III

I

Fool's Family Album

This is Fool's Crest smile,
stained with humble pie.

His license smile
on his learner's permit.

His blend-in smile,
somewhere in the picture.

His singles-bar smile,
after four Mai Tais.

His have-a-nice-day smile,
some read as "Kick me."

His may-I-help-you smile,
which scares the children.

His line-in-the-sand smile
and Chamberlain blink.

His who-me smile,
nimble as dead meat.

His my-turn smile,
if it's ever his turn.

His true-love smile,
lonely as Orion.

Fool's Paradise

Fool, who was standing too close when God
swept the rebel seraphim into perdition, tries,
as the former Lucifer exhorts, to make a heaven
of Hell. After all, feeling your eyeballs boil inside
keeps your mind off your smoldering testicles.
And there's practically no dress code, other than
that coat of film you get from the burning
bodily discharges. "This is great," he tells himself,
scalp bubbling. "Good as Heaven. Better."

He trades the key to his Heavenly treasure
to Moloch for a lighter pitchfork and membership
in the Gehenna Debating Society. He joins
the Woeful Chamber of Commerce, where he initiates
Bingo Night. When the morale of the damned rises
56 percent, he gives off-shore real estate a try.

But the now-Satan thinks he smells a power play,
and God's wrath rattles the cosmic chandelier
when half the cherubim start flying weekends
to some new spot called the Lake of Fire
Floating Oasis. The two hold secret talks
in a neutral galaxy, where, after a thousand years,
they negotiate a win-win solution.

Fool finds himself near the La Brea Tar Pits,
in the first of his innumerable earthly lives,
and Satan gets to use a gigantic flaming sword
to chase Adam and Eve out of Eden to a world
where they and their baffled descendants
are subject to sin, disease, insanity, and death,
all of which are invented for this occasion.
Fool takes a deep breath of miasma, feels groggy.
"This is great," he declares. "Couldn't *be* better."

Fool Expelled from Eden

OK, not *the* Eden, wasted on that pair
of gorgeous nitwits, but a pretty nice place
by Fool's lights, a little stucco number
tucked away in a little suburb bordered
by a mini-mall—just the spot to lever up
your dogs in the recliner and contemplate
the polka of the spheres, or so it seems
before the big rain washes away the stucco,
which is then discovered to be all
that keeps the house from turning into a pile
of reject lumber, which prompts Fool,
convinced he'd read the handwriting,
to invest in a discount ark franchise,
with easy credit from the pickpocket Time,
who, despite his oath to Fool, is always
on his own side and who, after shaking hands,
uses the old bump-and-snatch maneuver
to get Fool's skinny wallet and, after that,
his wife and four underachieving children,
and finally, his eyes, ears, nose, and brain,
which qualifies Fool for the X-tra Special
Olympics, where he loses to a Brazilian guy
down to sneering lips and a raised eyebrow.

Psycholinguistics

Trying to fix a flat in the bad end of the barrio,
Fool fumbles the jack, which lands
on his big toe, cranking up an air-raid siren
of pain. "FUCK," he blurts, surprised
by his profanity. What on earth has happened
to his angelic vocabulary? "SHIT," he adds,
and the howl relents a little. "Cocksucker,"
he continues, "motherfucker," at which
the gremlins of malaise draw back, holstering
their caltrops and roofing nails. "Why don't
you goddamned smegma-breathed, baboon-
butt-faced little fuck fuckers blow it
straight outta your blinky little assholes!"
he asks, which unfolds a conga line
of endorphins slow-kicking across
the reflective floors of his cerebrum,
thawing his grimace into a have-a-nice-day
smile. He feels like Ponce De Leon might have
if he'd discovered the Fountain of Youth
instead of an arrow sandwich. "Derringer
up my sleeve," he concludes, "balm
for the thousand cuts." He feels rain. "Fuckheads!
Pussy faces! Bite my dick!" he hollers at the drops,
slowing a low-rider loaded with shark eyes.

FOOL FOR LOVE

Fool finds himself smitten by a judge's daughter,
who's been reserved for someone like herself:
tycoon rich, Ivy League, Greekly statuesque,
and no fool. When he spotted her among the other
women on the planet, Fool's heart needed
high-powered binoculars just to see whether
she had blue eyes or brown. Fool imagines
that she loves old movies and city landscapes,
exactly as he does, that he's found his missing half
so he no longer has to stumble around on two left legs
like those down-the-middle amputees in *The Symposium*.
See the newly-rejoined on a balmy Union Square,
discussing the vault scene in *Citizen Kane*; in winter
see them snowball-sparring by the Flatiron Building,
in late spring dining on the Via Veneto. Divine
love, earthly love: fast as Chan and Eng? The calendar
flaps through the months as they choose the silverware,
coochie their first-born, . . . who looks away like Hitchcock
in a cameo.
        The iron park bench chills beneath the cloud
just abandoned by Fool's violins and French horns.
Is that hail?

Cabfare from the Airport

Buoyed by the start of his Caribbean holiday package,
Fool offers the driver too big a tip, which turns out
to be some sort of insult in this country. Fool doesn't
need to speak Spanish to get the picture, snarls being part
of a universal language, as is dropping a passenger off
in the part of town the police, whom almost everybody
fears, are afraid to stop in. Fool's money belt is full
of moths, but he looks like a dollar sign to the people
in this neighborhood. He asks a man with a flaming Jesus
tattooed on his back where the Hotel Paradiso is. When Fool
tries hand signals, the man thinks he is a rich homosexual
trolling for buggery.
                    The nurse in Intensive Care
hands Fool a waste basket to bleed in while he waits
for the doctor, who is also the mayor's nephew, which
is his only medical credential. Luckily, the doctor is out
on a three day bender and Fool's allowed to leave
after the bleeding stops and in exchange for his watch.
Fool walks the streets, sucking in breaths of supposedly
fresh air. "Yes!" he cries, botching a stutter-step.

Clothes Make the Fool

During Luau Day at Suit City,
Fool picks out a blue-serge number,
double-breasted, lapels down to his belt.

In the mirror, the sleeves and pant legs
look pretty short and the color a little too
liver. The thing itches, too, like horse hair.

The salesman says horse hair's coming back
and that all Fool needs to do is slouch an inch
or two and it'll fit good as a Brooks Brother.

Fool looks different now, like a penitent,
except his whole suit's made of hair.
Saint Anthony. Saint Jude. Saint Fool?

Buoyed, he ambles out, slouching and scratching
till he's mistaken by a mean cop for a lunatic
acting like a gorilla. Time for some skull music.

Fool ducks the billy and flees, gorilla style,
to a nearby bus, which empties before
he can dig the fare out of his hairy pocket.

The SWAT team's waited for something
really big like this since they were rookies.
They're thinking medals, TV movie.

Fool's shouts about sainthood and inseams
don't shield him from the fusillade of buckshot
and hollow point. The movie stars Fabio.

PLAYING THE FOOL

God makes Fool His Stratocaster. "Purple
Haze," He commands, and "Blue Hawaii" twangs
down to earth, creating Muzak, hemorrhoids,
and the Super Bowl halftime show. "Toccata
and Fugue," He says to Fool, His Wurlitzer,
and something akin to a 45 of "Tutti Fruiti"
played off-center descends, and with it forty wars,
smallpox, and the birth of Richard Nixon.

"OK," says God to Fool, his kazoo, "'Turkey
in the Straw,' anything," at which Heaven's
heavens crack apart from a high note worthy
of the cast from "Revelation," unleashing
Chaos and, with a blinding electrical pop,
Old Night. "Fine," says God. "Thanks for nothing."

Why Fool voted No-Nonsense

Because a spade
is a spade.

Because a spade
is not always a spade.

Because of what now
passes for love.

Because of what now
passes for jumbo.

Because of too much
footsie.

Because the news
is to blame.

Because of things
you're always hearing.

Because what's
the difference.

Because fools
are thicker than water.

The Consolation of Philosophy

Fool goes to visit his English cousin Foole,
an unemployed court jester, hoping to find
his roots. Foole, who's been waiting
since 1573 for the jester market to recover,
can't tell him a thing about their ancestors,
though they both doubt there'd be any dukes
or archbishops. Actually there are many,
plus seven kings, three saints, and the man
who invented aerosol cheese-spread. The two
go to a pub and drink till they turn philosophical.
"Is matter uniform or multiform?" asks Foole.
"Hume was right," posits Fool. "Cause and effect
is merely a perception." As each pint grows
a brighter halo, they grasp what all the fuss
over pure rational discourse is about.

The Right Stuff

On Fool's birthday, April 1, people play
jokes on him all day long. "April Fool!"
his wife and kids hoot as the pancakes explode.
"Gotcha again!" quips the gang at work
when he sits down in the Limburger cheese.
His mom and dad, though dead, always call to ask
if he has Prince Albert in a can. "Well, let him out!"
they shriek, not waiting for an answer.

By five o'clock, Fool feels like a space walker
cut loose from the mother ship. The radio
in his head chatters nonsense as he floats
end over end. "You are my sunshine,"
he sings *sotto voce*, "my only sunshine."

Lycanthropy

Even a man who is pure in heart
And says his prayers at night
May become a wolf when the wolf-bane blooms
And the autumn moon is bright.

After Fool's bitten by a large black dog,
he feels a brain-shorting urge to pee
on every bush he passes, pausing only
to sniff for turds. Raw human flesh
begins to sound downright tasty. Wait:
is that pentagram on his palm a bar stamp
or something a lot harder to rub off?
This only happens in movies, he thinks,
licking his balls as he scratches an ear
with a hind paw. The full moon silhouettes
a likely meal: a leggy, short-skirted babe
hurrying home through the park. He springs,
but instead of a mouthful of crimson pulchritude,
he gets a snout-full of pepper gas
and a spiked heel in the crotch. YIEEEEE,
he protests, rolling over. When she flashes
her badge and reads him his rights, he
tries hard to wish himself into a less
incriminating form. ACCOUNTANT! he wills
as she cuffs his front paws to his hind ones,
ACCOUNTANT! ACCOUNTANT! No dice.
He's booked for assault, indecent exposure,
and defecating on a public sidewalk. **Wolf's Clothes**
Can't Hide Sheep, quips the filler on page nine.

Basic Fool

"Get down and give me twenty!"
snaps Cupid. Fool pumps away,
boots burnished, seams crisp,
making choo-choo sounds.
"Show me your love face,"
snarls the cherub after Fool
wobbles to attention. "LOVE
FACE, maggot!" Cupid shrieks
as Fool mugs like a chimpanzee
having a stroke. Fool starts
to think he should have tried
something easier, like
fire-eating or celibacy.
After a night of introspection,
he hijacks a tank and drives
over Cupid, leaving a trail
of feathers and baby fat.
Later, he takes a high-speed
joyride in somebody's Porsche
with a waitress he's picked up.
"You may not believe this,"
Fool tells her right before
the blowout, "but I'm a flyboy
from the infantry of love."

Flight of the Fool, 1902

There was the wood-and-canvas number
with sixteen wings that folded up
on takeoff like a book slamming shut,
and the one topped with reciprocating

umbrella, which pumped itself
to scrap heap, and the rocket packet
on the back of ice-skating Fool, which
danced him into a crashing double-axel—

one by one, his inspirations
Maydayed down to sad kersplats.
Until today, when an oily pitchman
from Daedalus Hides and Elixirs sells him

their Motorized Pigskin Wings Kit
for three dollars a month, plus shipping
and handling. Using the easy-to-apply
assembly wax, Fool's ready for the wild

blue yonder in less than a week.
As he taxis down a hill, he feels the lift,
slight at first, then more, though he's headed
toward some telegraph wires. One

giant step for mankind, and one
dead pigeon, thinks Fool, who revs
for dear life as the wind thrusts him
toward a high-speed garroting. But then:

Look, up in the sky—it's Fool
banking unsteadily over the south end
of town, bringing good news
to the Smiths and Joneses, to the Third

National Bank and First Baptist Church,
to Grimm's Dry Goods and Payne's Dentistry:
Deliverance—every earthling free
as the bat-like apparition now attempting rolls

and figure-eights above the water tower.
Heaven's nearer, Fool plans to show
the meager crowd, who shade their eyes
and squint as he climbs toward the sun,

sputtering higher and higher till he's
a small black dot, then nothing,
and they, bemused for a moment,
turn back to their familiar avenues.

WISE FOOL

Fool's appointed the king's confidante
and resident goofball, the mental power
behind the throne, who speaks in jests
and riddles. This is a big responsibility,
thinks Fool. Say the wrong thing and
thwack. Even say the right thing
in a slightly wrong way and watch
the dominoes clatter into a black arrow
pointed straight at yours truly. So Fool
sticks to the chicken joke and the randy
tinker stories, laced with a couple
of mossy ballads, hoping nobody
will end up paying much attention
to any of it, though he finds himself
hailed for the kingdom's "Golden Year."
The "to get to the other side" line alone
turns an army revolt into a fife concert.
Imagine Fool's surprise and relief,
till they need a beloved celebrity
to burn for the smallpox epidemic.

SHIP OF FOOL

is a bathtub toy of Chance, who loves to play
Torpedo, Typhoon, Big Silent Iceberg;
who sings, "Fwim, wittle fishies, fwim if you can,"
when the body count gets good and the cries
swarm up like fizz in a Shirley Temple.
Lashed to the wheel in his yellow slicker,
Fool dead reckons the way, aiming
a weather eye at the horizon, where clouds
hairy as wolf-pack captains flash signals
and close in. "Steady as she goes," he commands
while the last rat belly-flops for Frisco.

Fool thinks the odds should keep his sloop,
with its busty good-luck figurehead,
from going down *every* time it touches water.
He wonders about the smell of urine
and Mr. Bubble that wafts in after
each new launching. He just wonders.

FOOL ELECTRIC

Sparks sing though Fool's arteries
and veins; synapses flash. When he
passes parking lots, rows of cars
start up, their alarms yammering.

Winos spontaneously combust. At the mall,
pacemakers spike, computers spout gibberish,
floor buffers juke through crowds
like Packer fullbacks. Two cops give chase,

seething beneath their instant clown-wigs.
As Fool flees past a funeral home,
the deceased lurches up from her satin mattress,
then struts down the aisle and out the door,

like a majorette at the FedEx Orange bowl.
The late news asks if Fool could be Jesus,
back to give every Christian family
their own Lazarus. Polls show 97 per cent

of Americans now believe in a loving God,
the remaining three percent intent on
fleeing the country. Fool can hardly believe
his luck—a mission for his Eveready heart:

to zap death where it doesn't just hurt
and make electric whoopee with the world.
Soon the dead parade down every street,
drawing smiles of recognition, giving off

good cheer with every puff of ozone
till it's noticed they walk ka-dunk, ka-dunk,
like zombies, and gaze without a spark of interest
at even the hors d'oeuvres and good silver. Worse,

they can't hold a charge, listing left
or right, hair a fright, breath blinky,
their telltale buzz sounding lower and lower,
till they drop on the street or right at the table,

creating, though well-dressed, an eyesore
and health hazard, reminding everyone
of a subject still best avoided in polite company.
On the lam again, Fool ducks into the gas works.

FOOL AND HIS MONEY

Shooting for promotion to archangel, Fool draws
a name out of a hat to sponsor a mortal in need
of Divine guidance. The office wise-asses
rig it so he gets Adolf Hitler, whom Fool,
having drunk too deep from the Heavenly cooler,
decides could benefit greatly from mastering
basic listening-skills. Incarnated, he tells
the Fuherer's receptionist at the Reichstag
that, despite what his cowlick and too-small
Monkey Ward three-piece might suggest,
he comes from On High, that term delivering Fool
a little shiver of confidence. In the basement,
Gestapo agents hook his bruised testicles up
to a crank telephone. "Calling Leipzig," Hans
quips to Dieter, anteing two longs and a short.

As Fool's heart beats a retreat into his small
intestine, he's forced to consider evil's toehold
on the world, which he hasn't seemed to loosen
even slightly, which he might be tightening,
his defenselessness tempting the depraved
to reach for that extra 10 percent. He wishes
he'd had some kind of handbook to consult,
one with a good index—but, no, nothing
but a couple of cyanide breath-mints and a note
that reads, "Inspected by Number 17."

Where's all that Omniscience, Omnipotence,
and Everlasting Concern for employee safety,
wonders Fool between jolts, persevering still
around hope's steeplechase. After he dies
for us in this and several other wide shots
at guardian-angelship, Fool's put in charge
of the Small Consolations detail that plants
dimes and quarters under sofa cushions.
Each one you find contains his blessing.

WORLD'S BIGGEST FOOL

At the doctor's, Fool notices his weight's up
almost half a ton. No wonder his jeans cut
and his old shoes pinch so. He gets a new outfit

at a big-men's store, which helps till he puts on
another two tons. The tabloids show an interest,
but Fool finds himself thinking big,

hatching ideas that wouldn't have squeezed
into his normal-sized head, now larger
than a Big Boy statue's. "Is the pleasure of the pig

as great as the pleasure of the philosopher?"
he asks the mailman, feeling concepts
roll though his mind like happy sea-otters.

He begins to see through the pea soup
of everydayness, then through corduroy,
then oak tables. His doctor says it must be

a nervous affliction, brought on by
chronic ineptitude and water retention.
He prescribes strong diuretics and two weeks

in the Caymans. But Fool's grown too big
to fit inside a plane or atop a cruise ship.
He acquires his own field of gravity,

then bounds through the ionosphere
and into space, where he takes his place
as the ninth planet in our solar system. China

draws up plans to colonize him, the CIA
to terminate him with extreme prejudice. Now
God has to admit Fool's jammed the gears

again, making life difficult for Everybody,
another word He uses to mean Himself. Meanwhile,
Fool's discovered the missing link, the lost chord,

the cure for cancer and old age, and devised
the half-hour work week. He's really, really
big now, too big to kill with a bolt of lightning

or the old pillar-of-salt stunt. Fool's heart
takes up a galaxy. There's room in it
for all humankind, even burdens on society

and threats to public decency. Everybody,
which, of course, includes God, now adrift
inside that humongous ticker, flushed

from auricle to ventricle, awash in the blood
of a fool. Out goes sin, out goes death.
In comes the free pass and the truly

bottomless Margarita—which
set off God's Doomsday Device for when
life gets too good for our own good.

BANG goes the whole shebang, leaving God
back at square one. "OK, Goddamn it,"
He sighs. "From the top: Let there be light . . .

blah, blah, blah." Back on earth, Fool,
reincarnated to his old size and kick-me grin,
grabs a fig leaf and tries to look busy.

II

MY FATHER'S LAUGH

It was a bursting, like when the cap
comes off a boiling radiator. He'd buckle
and turn red; big tears would runnel
down his cheeks, drip off his nose.

It took tits to bring it on, bazooms,
or idiots or feet doing their stuff
or a drunk taking a cross-eyed fall
into a six-tiered wedding cake.

It took Red Skelton or Jerry Lewis
or me one day with my new-bought
Whoopee Cushion, making blats
and peeps for him, tootles and flaps.

He couldn't stop till I did, a turnaround
from the times he'd catch me in his sights,
finger jabbing home those points
about straightening up and flying right.

I was bursting too, his begotten son,
his Siamese twin, busting a gut,
he'd say, laughing my ass off—the two of us
funny as a rubber crutch.

THE PALMER METHOD

The penmanship drill became an exercise in confomity.
That's what [educators] thought would be a good idea.
—Tamara Plakins Thornton,
Handwriting in America: A Cultural Study

Above the blackboards, its stately letters
minueted clear around the room, remote
and immutable as Ursa Major or the Flag.
You had to keep your pen from snagging
in the chippy paper with its triple lines
to guide like training wheels. You had to
practice rows of spirals—slanting
smartly to the right—till they uncoiled
uniformly as a clock spring. You had to
measure up, it urged, or stay a scrawler,
a sad sack whose droopy Rs and nervous Js
could kill your chances for success and love,
whose checks might come back branded
"Insufficient Capital." With a pen stroke,
you could find yourself consigned to mail clerk
living alone in some bare-walled walk-up,
block letters on your set of rubber stamps.

PANTSING BOBBY FREEMAN
IN FIFTH GRADE

It could have been the asthma spray
   or the Cub Scout shoes; maybe his sluggy
      opalescence or just the eyes that said

"free shot." When I got there
   they'd pushed him down behind
      the bushes near the school's back door,

yanked off the baggy corduroys,
   then the Jockeys, which had Shmoos
      on the elastic, and flung them

up onto a low branch, the Jockeys
   waving in the May breeze, flashing
      their little brown spot like a flag

of unconditional exposure. "Eeeyow,
   shit stains!" somebody yelled,
      as Bobby squirmed to cover up

his tiny pecker and those eyes,
   and I joined in a ballsy-toned guffaw,
      one like I'd heard my father share,

matching boilermakers
   with his buddies from the plant—
      one B-flick Viking to another

as the monastery roars. It felt OK,
   and school so nearly out.

Scouts in Wilderness

In a pile of beer cans near a swollen creek, they took us
by surprise: grownups old as our parents,
grimly stunting on the backs of playing cards,
in garter belts and argyle socks, oily
curls and oddly placed tattoos. The best one,
someone called it, showed two plump women standing
spread-legged, each with her hand hoisting the other's
slackened breast. Before them sat a man,
back to camera, who'd taken the cord from a tassel-
shaded lamp and plugged it between the legs
of the taller one, who didn't seem to get the joke.

The lamp glowed on what we'd heard women
had down there, in that unknown they never
showed in *Photography* or *Gent*, but broadcast here
up close, faraway, and in-between;
solo, duet, trio, allez-ooped
in grainy permutations we swapped, shuffled,
and swapped again each night, whose mothers
would have cried, "Don't touch!" that no one knows
where they've been, what horny, cankered hand
dealt them to babies earning merit badges.
We kept them for a week, then turned them in
to the highway patrol, who said they'd start a file.

Home again, deep in our rooms, we'd watch
till sleep as those ghostly tumblers, going through
the motions for a crowd of rubes, arranged themselves
into clumsy letters, spelling some foreign word.

PRODIGY

"Here's your accordion," smirks the assistant devil
in the cartoon where Hell's appalled draftees
receive their instruments. No one told me
in sixth grade, the day I instantly made music
in the accordion "ensemble" the piano store
formed to move some merchandise. Four notes
up and down, with a bass shift at the top,
something a retarded chimp could slap out
for a sugar treat, something my mother pronounced
a gift from God: her little Paganini playing
with one foot in the New York Philharmonic.

She bought it, so did I, till the lessons started,
my teacher, Mr. Lemke, chewing his lip
as I wheezed my way through the first three books,
"Lady of Spain" harumphing beyond my grasp
and drowned out in my head by Chuck and Elvis.

Mother dragged me out before her squarest guests
to sulk and fumble through her favorites.
I was being baby-stepped toward Lawrence Welk,
the anti-Christ of Rock 'n' Roll, who played
that anti-matter of the Fender Strato. "Once more,"
they'd say, as I hit the stage in my killer ducktail,
pumping a D where a B flat should have been.

Balsa

It came before those plastic parts
whose finished edges go together
like heels snapping to attention:
the wood that wouldn't, with its nasty
hints of what my elders hadn't
told me, that sometimes what looks
so ready to be shaped into a Stuka
or a Mustang, a battleship, at least
a cruiser, won't cut right however
sharp or cunning your X-Acto,
will crack and splinter, snap
and crush, will steer your blade
off the mark and into your finger
as you try to trace the filigreed
imprints stamped on those blocks
and sheets with their curt
instructions to "cut along edges"
or "carve canopy and nacelles
from block provided." I was
the maker, it the old mishap
twixt cup and lip, twixt reach
and butterfingered grasp. I tried
and tried, before I boxed up
the skeletal remains and stuck them
deep in our basement closet.

Bully

On our block, his side of the street
was his side of the street, this big kid,
a stunted Teddy Roosevelt patrolling
San Juan Hill, who'd lurk in his driveway
till you crossed that imaginary line
he'd scored along the curb. The gut punch
bent you double, seized your breath,
left no marks. Sometimes his father
would look on from the porch,
long face neutral as a referee's
or a loaded .45, a can of Pabst
sweating in his hand. I crossed over
more than once, not quite sure why,
disgruntled peon taking on United Fruit.
I'd run home crying to my parents,
who'd get right on the phone to say,
"See here," halfheartedly. "See here."

Coach Said

no water during practice. You don't wanna end up
like the guys in those movies, lost for days
in the desert and then they find the oasis and guzzle
away with nobody there to stop em. They think
their luck's finally changed, that the world's just
turned into Momma's tit, but they get water-logged
and die. I saw a man die in the war—bang, like that—
the start of training, run over by the bus that brought us,
and I don't want to see it again, no sir. It can spoil
a good marriage, seeing that. So don't let me find
anybody sneaking water. Use the salt tablets. And no
dissipation the night before a game—"shooting your wad"
to you comedians in the back. It drains vital fluids,
same as crying. You're left with an unfocused mind
and a case of cotton mouth. Take some extra laps if
you're so hot and bothered. Jump in a cold whirlpool.
Don't expect to be some Romeo stud, who thinks
his little cheerleader won't spit on him when he's down.
I could tell you some things, but just remember this:
It ain't gonna be like last year. No goddamn water.

WOW

We were these three high-school
yo-yos cruising along a county road
one boring Sunday afternoon
in my friend Bill's '52 Chevy coupe,
a car that didn't interest girls
or even us too much because,
among other shortcomings,
it only had six cylinders,
though it could go nearly 100,
which, because of slackened
minds, blue balls, and Chuck Berry
playing "School Days"
on station WOW's Top Twenty,
was how fast we were going,
when, in the words of news items
about traffic fatalities,
the driver lost control,
despite what I now remember
as a road straight and flat
as a runway. Oh well. So
there we were: sitting quietly
on the beltless bench-seats
as the car whipped around
like the Tilt-A-Whirl at Playland Park,
spinning toward the ditch
on our right, closer and closer
for one of those moments
expansive enough to contain
that well-known highlight film

of your life. But nobody seemed
to be reviewing his. Instead,
we glanced at one another,
like Beaver and Wally and Lumpy
trying to be polite by letting
someone else be the first to rise
from the table or like the 3 guests
on the TV quiz show *To Tell
The Truth*, when they would
try to tease the audience
after host Bud Collier
concluded the game by saying,
"And now, will the *real*
Ira Gershwin please stand up,"
with each of us remaining seated
in the still-spinning Chevy,
waiting to see how this episode
of his life would turn out,
whether the real him
would stand up and not
just a transparent image
like Robert Sterling and Anne Jeffreys
got stuck with when they died
in the car wreck at the beginning
of *Topper*, each of us occasionally
glancing out his own TV
-sized window at what looked like
one of those scenes where
Peter Gunn's been slipped

a Micky and they're trying to use
the camera to show how it feels
—till, at last, the car, minus a tire,
the muffler, and two kick-ass
'55 Olds spinner hubcaps,
gouged to a stop at the edge
of the road and, feeling both
like transparent images and real
high-school yo-yos, we stepped
out and walked around it,
the front end of which slumped
like Mr. Gillespie did when
we didn't practically shit our pants
during the gory film he showed us
in driver's ed. "Wow," we said,
cocking our heads and hooking
our thumbs in the pockets of our Levi's
like the transparent image of that coolest
of traffic fatalities, James Dean. "Man."

Speed

If you don't crash now and then,
you don't know how fast you can go.
—Dave Aldana, Motorcycle Hall of Famer

It drew Bandini and Von Trips
to kingdom come at Monza and Monaco,
and Vuckovich at Indy, and my high school pals

into a mountain outside Denver (morticians
couldn't tell whose parts were whose).
Speed—the pull of it, the blur, the white,

white rush inside that pocket of velocity,
where past and future plume off behind
like shreds of that contract

with your better brain as you hurtle
toward the vanishing point. And, yes,
that Brit, Moss, had it right: it's the curves,

not the straightaways, "having a bloody go"
at the "absolute limit of tyre adhesion,"
eyes, brain, muscle pressed into the arc,

like a painter stroking the perfect line,
like a safecracker when the tumblers click.
Like a stray soul plunged into bright water

and delivered: Jesus!

Rental Tux

It chafed like some new skin we'd grown,
or feathers, the cummerbund and starched collar
pinching us to show how real this transformation
into princes was, how powerful we'd grown
by getting drivers' licenses, how tall and total
our new perspective, above that rusty keyhole
parents squinted through. We'd found the key:
that nothing really counts except a romance
bright as Technicolor, wide as Cinerama,
and this could be the night. No lie.

Movie with the Guys, 1956

You're about the purdiest woman around these parts—I think.
—James Dean as Jett Rink in *Giant*

It's Jett Rink's final scene, in a big big-D hotel,
where he's arranged his coronation, which everyone's
walked out of. He's at the dais table in his rumpled tux,
face in his plate, snorfing into the mike

he tipped over when he passed out on shots. "Poor Jett,"
his amplified voice booms around the hall. "Poor Jett,"
it whines because no one's ever said it, or will, not even
his one true love, who looks just like Elizabeth Taylor

because she is Elizabeth Taylor, or her fat-cat hubby,
Rock Hudson, who seems more interested in the vaqueros,
or her dim-bulb daughter, who Jett was going to settle for,
though she doesn't look a thing like Elizabeth Taylor.

Can you hear the cry, Daphne O'Dwyre, who told me
the perfume I bought you with my French Club dues
smelled like bug spray and whined to me about your parents
grounding you for the junior prom, only to show up

in the back seat of that shithead Danny Larkin's
Merc for practically the whole school to see, leaving me
with a wilted purple nosegay and a rental tux
that smelled like cat piss and Lysol? Poor Jett.

Naked in Public

I'm back in that glass phone-booth
in the mega-mall, the one about the size
of Houston, feeling that familiar draft
where my wallet ought to be, that familiar need
to improvise. I'd have wished
for fewer shoppers, but it's Absolute
Clearance Day, everything marked down
to free of charge, and Elvis has resurfaced here
for his farewell concert. He's wearing
that baby-blue outfit. Trying to dial Apparel
on the pillowy tot-phone, I wonder
if the stores are out of underpants. Overcoats.
Sheets. Shoe boxes. Could I scrounge
enough Scotch tape and sales slips
to rig a pair of briefs? Outside the booth,
the Registrar certifies my degrees
as void, what with my cutting
that whole semester of Developmental
Long Division. I remember now: the big
fat F. Shoving through the undistracted throng,
brown-toothed Bernie Sindelar, who liked to
beat me transcendental after school,
announces it was all a misunderstanding,
that he had me mixed up with somebody he hated.
I duck and cover beneath my desk
at Coolidge Junior High, trying to divide 435
by x, bare cheeks aquiver as the P.A. barks,
"This is not a drill. This is not a drill."

Antique Classic

I'm looking for a '50 Mercury,
two-door coupe,
metallic heliotrope,
shaved, chopped, and channeled
till it's turret shaped and serpent eyed;
with Lake pipes, Olds spinners,
Hilburn-injected Chrysler hemi
cammed with an Isky Crossflow 7000.

I want to rumble
slowly through my past,
pressing my bicep
against the door, looking
pathetic with my white whiskers
and Metamucil. I'll slump
over the wheel, receiving
and concealing, a Lucky
above my left ear,
and let that hemi
back-off past the gym,
where it echoes, like I used to
see Bernie Lapinski do
Friday nights after the football game,
when my lonely pals
and I followed the crowd
downtown to Tiner's Drive-In
for noise and posturing,
for sugar and salt
and a look at Debby Conroy

waltzing from car to car, taking
orders, leaving us
dreams too lush
to talk about; and for a look
at Bernie's Mercury,
burnished, anointed,
whose turning-in
proclaimed the heart
of the city, of the world,
had once more shifted
to Forty-sixth and Dodge.

But Bernie packed a grudge
sprung like a switchblade,
and Debby was reserved
for a Coupe de Ville. You could
look but couldn't touch:
her ivory face, Bernie's
fierce Merc, the past
already rumbling off.

Obedience

The ghost of it whimpered back last night
from a wet November fifty years ago:
a scraggly cocker that shadowed me home
from school and, when I let it in, ignored
a meal to snuffle crotches and hump legs
as if to win us with what it knew of love,
its sad pink dick unsheathed like a gut
protruding from a wound, its rheumy eyes
spinning with dread, its odor of mushroom
and shit making itself at home in our carpet.

"No. Bad dog. Down," we said, shoving it away
till my father got it in the car, and we drove off
through the dark to a cornfield outside town,
where the rain blew and it slumped off right away,
going to get lost, like a good dog.

School Lesson

Is there one in everybody's attic: that photo
of our fifth-grade class, from which Miss Blair
still monitors the week, and our classmate
Linda, third row, second from the right,
offers the slightest smile from the spring before
she went home in the middle of the day and stayed
for three whole weeks and then, they told us,
simply died? We barely knew her, always
seated several rows behind us or standing
on the far side of the playground, vague
reflection in the corner of our eye, her house
beyond our neighborhood. Afterwards there came
a certain shift of light, a tilting in the landscape
everywhere. We didn't comprehend,
eventually forgot, till Ed, a high-school buddy,
missed a curve and spun his Studebaker
through a power pole. We signed the book, went stiffly
through his funeral, walking like our parents.

The Art of Motorcycle
Maintenance

You've got to find somebody
who can smell a loose bolt
or a brake cable going bad,
who has a slight stutter
or tic and several black fingernails,
who works in a cinder-block building
just off River Street, its air brusque
with the fumes of 50-weight, hi-test,
and Lucky Strikes; a place with dark
recesses, a rust-stained toilet, and a sign
that reads "Bobby's Cycle." Leave
your bike with Bobby. Let him tune it
like a concert grand, perfecting
its voice, touching it like a safecracker,
whispering now and then
till the shafts settle into balance,
fluids topped, the engine quivering
precisely on middle C. He won't like you
very much, or any other human
machine, because people can't blend
like a set of well-synched carbs
or the pistons on a big quad.

You've got to lose somebody:
little you, with that Cub Scout sense
of gravity and motion, those phobias
of borderlines and letting go. The borders
in this state are paradoxical and stern
as Herzegovina's: steer left and you

veer off to the right; stare at that box
that just fell off the truck in front of you
and you'll hit it square as if you'd aimed;
stiffen up in danger, *struggle* to regain
control, and you'll invite an overthrow
that could be final. The thing is,
as the analysts say in chorus,
to relax and focus on the bright side,
on the place you *want* to go,
not on the dark spot near
the pavement's edge, or on that crack
your boss made about a transfer
to Paducah. Quit brooding on the high speed
wobble, the endo, a decline in futures.
Have faith in the sturdy god of gyroscopics
and, despite the October chill, this tangy day
when you're not yet dead or worse. Think
of your old fox terrier, snoot thrust gladly
out the window of the Galaxy. Think
of when, stretching out your arms and running
down a hill, you were flying, flying.

Class of '59

Here we are, called back
for an August weekend
of bag -wine and buffet,
the ones alive who chose
to answer. And here
we are, ten years older
than our parents were
when we sashayed off to find
a life, when time was just
a joke on them.

We've arrived, in the Orient
Room, Ramada West,
road weary, adjusted
for the cost of living, past
the need to care who knows
how high we've climbed
or had to jump, a few
nearly as trim and fresh
as I remember, another few
distorted into strangers, the rest
mostly recognizable
after a moment,
like when we had to guess
who matched those baby pictures
in the yearbook. Thank God
for the big name tags.

We muster smiles as we try
to read between the lines
and wattles. *This must
be you. This must be me*, we muse,
surprised we're not unhappy,
showing our age,
showing our class,
lifting our plastic cups.

III

Pity the Fool

Fool decides he'll try to make his disadvantage
work for him by playing on people's sympathies,
like Chaplin did as the lovable Little Tramp.
He spends the last of his savings on a frazzled bowler
and an oversized pair of shoes, starts walking
like a penguin, and is surprised to discover
that meek-looking little tramps might as well
be wearing kick-me signs. Some drivers
swerve to hit him as they pass. Doe-eyed girls,
who ought to respect a little vulnerability in a man,
stroll right by with their bruisers. When he lands
a job as greeter at a Wal-Mart, a little old lady
throws him a forearm-to-the-chest before he can
thank her for shopping there. The manager
fires him on the spot and then has him arrested
for trespassing. As they cuff him, he wishes he'd
saved enough for the endearing baggy pants.
"Watch your head," says the attending officer,
giving it a good bang on the squad-car door.

Fools Give You Reasons

Back in the Celestial City for another reassignment,
Fool's anxious to discuss his misadventures
with all the old friends and inside connections
he wishes he had. The people at the office,
where his desk is now occupied by a high-powered
shredder, are too busy to hear about Hitler
or Wal-Mart or the angry poor. They're planning
a surprise birthday party for God, forgetting again
that He's omniscient, He's always been born,
and they're but a dim blip in His Plenitude.
So they don't want to hear Fool's blather
about the storm of suffering on the universe's
model planet. They're sorry, but the Theology
Department's two buildings down. They like to think
of themselves as facilitators, the ones who polish
those crystalline gears the system rides on,
and are humble enough to admit they couldn't say
exactly what that means. There's no time to suffer
fools here. No time, period.

FOOLISH TEARS

Fool makes tear floods to go with his sigh tempests
and mind quakes when he thinks of all the world's
blown gaskets and loose rods, how its bent frame
wobbles through the cosmos like a junker Olds
with a couple of blowouts, how its six billion passengers
bump along in sorrow and hope and terror and sometimes
that sweet jalopy called love. Tonight, Fool's sobs
blort through the dark as dogs bark and big rigs
blast across the overpass. He wonders why he was born
so many times and what's the use of being
such a big crybaby out here bedded in a flop house
doorway, sparring with plastic bags, waving
as the young sweep by in splendor's rental limo.

FOOL DEMONSTRATES
HIS INVENTION

"It explodes like roses,
laughter, birth," says Fool,
touching off five green sparks
that flash to sunbursts
and vault into the night,
where they bloom
and blam and shower.
He says celebrations
will never be the same,
that he can form the stuff
into candles, snakes, cherries.

"Think of the children,
their upturned faces
shimmering in the dark,"
says Fool. "Think
of the stubbornest obstacles
blown away," he says
to the Emperor,
who's already thinking.

Fool Noir

It felt like every other night in this crummy town,
like you'd been cold-cocked and stuffed in a dumpster,
like when a pet-store ferret crawls up your pant leg
and bites you in the balls, like when you've sloshed in
wet cement and don't know it till you see the tracks
on your new carpet, yeah, and then see darker tracks,
from when you set your sock on fire trying to light
a cigarette the way Bogie did in *The Maltese Falcon*
and danced hitch-kick flambé around the living room,
knocking Dad's ashes off the mantle and into the fondu
you put out for the big party nobody but the cops
showed up for. Yeah, business as usual in dullsville
—till *she* walked in, but that's another story. Yeah.

Ninety-seven-pound Fool

Shades cocked on his forehead, Fool spreads
his beach towel on the sugar-crystal sand,
smoothes out the wrinkles for his Felicity,
hoists a beach umbrella. This is the life, he thinks
as he eases onto the tie-died terry cloth. Just then,
the bully Act struts by, kicking sand on them.
Fool's protests earn him two black eyes,
and Felicity strides off with the assailant.

Browsing at the drugstore, Fool finds an ad
for the Charles Atlas body-building system
on the back of a comic book and, after applying
Dynamic Tension for only fifteen minutes a day,
swells into an image of the founder. Adonis-ized,
he marches to the beach to win back his beloved,
only to find she's taken up with Thought,
a yachtsman, whose charm is unassailable,
whose marble library is all Greek to Fool.

THE JUGGLER

Fool starts with three red balls, tossing them up
like fountain water, first two-handed, then one.
It feels good, natural, but too easy, so he
tries behind the back, between the knees,
over the shoulder. Child's play. He's got a knack,
he thinks, a calling. But he needs to stretch.
He tries two chairs and a table, then a pole lamp
and two radios, then four cleavers and a hatchet.
Finally, he does the one he saw on *Believe It or Not*:
three chain saws on full razz. A cinch, so he adds
another, plus an ocelot and two bicycles. He's
on a roll now. Up go a Shetland, a Clydesdale,
a widow and her banker. Not enough,
so: the New York Philharmonic, Hoover Dam,
Neptune, Jupiter. It's cosmic now, celestial,
which brings in God, Who's not too pleased
at such levity encroaching on His grandeur.
Zap, Fool finds himself empty-handed,
waking from a dream his analyst will say
symbolizes masturbation, though Fool still feels
the heavenly wheeling, the lift and catch,
the windswept to and fro, dam after planet, she
after he, gravity become Fool's blithe assistant
in a skirt so short you can see to Pago Pago.

FOOL RUSHES IN

Fool joins the California gold rush
and strikes, of course, fool's gold,
which he thinks might have been
named after him, like Pike's Peak
was named after, well, that guy. He feels
very honored till he tries to pay
a prostitute with some and the madam
shoots the top half of his ear off.
He has trouble hearing after that
and is later hanged by a posse
who thinks he's someone else,
who's also missing half an ear.
"Eh?" he kept answering.

That's Entertainment

Thanks to the grudge against Howitzer Films
of its soon-to-be-fired personnel director,
Fool gets a job creating major motion pictures.
A committee gathers around a huge table,
like bankers or statesmen. At each place
sits a bottle of Poland Springs, a legal pad,
and a monogramed pen set, with blotter.
Members talk about AFTRA and BAFTA.
They say "boff" and "hotsy" and "I'm just thinking
out loud, now." Fool mimics the wallpaper till he
picks up the jargon. "That's not in our wheelhouse,"
he chimes in. "We need to hit a zeitgeist."
Triggered now, he says he likes the classic
Army training films—their edgy dialogue, their
grainy authenticity. Others smirk and roll their eyes,
till the studio head declares the idea "retro chic,"
a term he heard on a recent *Jeopardy.* "This is it,
people," he says, "It's D Day, it's Lassie." The others
quickly come to see Fool's mismatched sideburns,
Brut cologne, and nasal vowels as a show
of ultra coolness. After their flurry of verbal knees
and elbows to get near his jittery right hand,
the new blockbuster concept is delivered:
V.D. II: the Final Chapter—They Thought!,
starring Fool, J Lo, the 2008 women's Olympic
beach volleyball team, and the producer's son-in-law.
Leading the salute as they run that baby up the flagpole,
Fool thinks genius smells like buttered popcorn.

FOOLIN' AROUND

God decides to put someone dull and loyal
in temporary charge and take a much-needed
vacation. "Stay put and don't touch *anything*,"
He tells Fool, then leadfoots His platinum
Hummer to Vegas, where you get free drinks
if you gamble. The rear bumper says, "If you
can read this, you're salt." Fool's not about
to touch something, being now an *omnipotent*
klutz. But he can't resist trying to pick up
the Hammer of Creation, which causes him
to stumble against the Divine Trash Bin,
spilling Hate and Death into the Pipeline,
which schleps them back into the fabric
of temporal life, where there'll be hell
to pay, Fool knows, being omniscient also.

Hate and Death collide with an Earth perfected
through love, science, and blunders, closing
the Festival of Cushy Jobs with Free Lunches,
the Madness, War, and Cancer Museum,
the 20 or 500? Age Guessing Jamboree.
Tragedy vaults back above comedy in the canon,
and, his hour come round at last, maple-eyed
little Adolph becomes a real boy again.

DICKHEAD

In what he mistook
for a fitness magazine,
Fool discovers the secret
of the penis: size
is everything.

He orders an enlarger
from a company called
Impossible Dream
Hydraulics.
It pumps him up
to bratwurst size, then
provolone, and,
with the last attachment,
retarded Siamese twin.

He doesn't know
how he'll find a dance card
long enough to match,
whether he's *too* large
for the goddess Renown.

He waits weeks by the phone,
rehearsing answers to *People*
and *O*, wondering
why he no longer cares
any more about humankind
than does his bald companion,
which remains absorbed

in its simple calisthenics
and which he's come to resemble
around the brow.

The Perfect Fool

After his umpteenth failure to spot a red herring
when it slaps him in the face, Fool's coat turns
the colors of all the world's spills, his cap rises
to an irrefutable point. The sum of his gaffs
equals the square root of his misconceptions.
Stay back if you value your toes. Keep him
off your boat. Wherever he goes, keystones
fracture, the law of gravity teeters on repeal.

Every month his house makes the cover
of *Before* magazine. His Yugo's the envy
of the trendier scrap yards. Thanks to him,
the common step-ladder now boasts thirty
caution stickers. The ABA would name him
Plaintiff of the Year, if he'd only sue.
But he's too foolish, grief's warm-up bag,
unhygenically pure, who might love anyone.

Seismic

On damp days, Fool's feet pick up
   vibrations from the dead, who still want
      answers, who've been on hold too long.

They're not *that* dead, they insist, voices
   crowding up like bubbles in a boiling pot.
      Fool steps gingerly as they carry on

about loaded dice and thumbs on the scales,
   bum wiring and worse plumbing,
      cracks and leaks, fizzles and ruptures.

But it's not all grief down there. Sometimes
   they sing: "Roll Me Over," for example, or,
      in stormy weather, "Stormy Weather."

Today, they aim a Bronx cheer
   at what makes the flesh so fickle,
      but too many tongues fall out

or are already gone, which leads
   to a brief dirge of bone clatter
      that they flip to a marimba-band take

on "Jumpin' Jack Flash." "But it's all right now,"
   they sass, "in fact it's a gas," which makes Fool
      look both ways and try a little strut.

The Fool Tree

Poof! Like that,
he's rooted thirty feet
into the seventh green,

feeling the chilly nudge
of worms, the tickle
of mole whiskers and

assorted cilia. Has he
blown his birdie? Where
did his five iron go?

Where, for God's sake,
did his arms, his eyes, his
you-know-what?

Maybe he should have tried
a mashie. Does Blue Cross
cover acute rooting?

He doesn't care. *Why
move from this spot*
he wonders, *ever?*

*Why not dine
on the seasons? Waltz
in the tuck of breezes?*

Tango in gales?
His skin's gnarled

hard enough to blunt

any slur or worry.
His twiggy pate
will leaf out

every year. *Tall,*
he muses, *Ancient,*
Anchored, Majestic,

his thick bark deaf
to the chain saw's
choke and rattle.

Alone No More

It's Berlin right after *Krystallnackt*,
and Fool needs someone he can talk to,
someone to share his downs and
really downs. He settles for a parrot,
a green and yellow macaw he's told
speaks only Yiddish. "*Schmuck*!" it says
when he laments the water over the dam,
the money down the drain. "*Putz!*"
it barks over the upset apple carts
and spilt milk. The Groucho smile
on its beak leads Fool to look up
those words, and then some others.
"*Momzer!*" he fires back, "*Kucker!*"

Fool feels they've found a droll way
of expressing mutual affection,
maybe love. "*Nebish,*" they squawk
at one another over a shared walnut.
It's a fair swap for the human touch,
he's thinking when the Gestapo shows up
on a tip from his snoopy neighbor.
Schmendriks! Fool shouts as a welcome
to these strangers in black leather coats,
who know Jew talk when they hear it.

DANSE MACABRE

*But Death, acting the part of a messenger, naturally
took to the attitude and movement of the day, namely
the fiddlers and other musicians, and the Dance of Death
was the result.*
—The Catholic Encyclopedia

It's ladies' choice tonight, guys along the east wall,
gals along the west as the cruise ship *False Hope*
lists to starboard. Adjusting his Jockeys, Fool tries
to remember the difference between the fox trot

and the hundred-meter dash, while crooner
Don Ho spoons out "Beautiful Kaua'i"
on the turn table Death filched from the DJ's room
after tempting him to jump overboard, leaving

a note scrawled in Danish someone translated as,
"The silence of God mocks our leaping sex horse
struggle." When couples form, Death puts on
an oldie line-dance called "The Madison."

"When I say hit it," he says, "I want you to go
two up, two back, double cross, and come out of it
with the Swim. Hit-a-it." Immersed now in the days
when time was languid as water in the shallow end,

everyone but Fool comes out of it doing
that standup Australian crawl. "You're look-kin
good," Death says, slicking back his hairpiece.
As Fool's partner huffs to the powder room,

water blasts through the portholes, causing
everyone to stroke for dear life. "Hold fast
to me," Fool burbles to Death, who's dolphining off
to his next gig. "I was nearly an Eagle Scout."

The Incredible Shrinking Fool

Mountain lion! thinks Fool, just before he sees
it's Snuggles. When he stands, he's eye-to-eye
with the TV. The carpet pile's ankle deep,

moving toward his shins. "EEK," he Minnie Mouses,
music to Snuggles, who hears an evening meal
in the pile of clothes where his master stood.

Fool's now lost in the Grand Canyon
of his left loafer. 9 D, say colossal imprints
on the east wall, which smells like feet.

Then he falls through the molecules
of the sole, through a hydrogen atom,
then a quark, till he's a nano-step from God,

who, unknown to many, is infinitely small
as well as large and wise and good
and never to be told he seems

a lot taller in the Bible or on TV,
as Fool remarks. But, since infinitely small
implies nonentity, God feels free here

not to act the big shot, even suggests
Fool call him Peewee and play him
in a round of miniature golf. Tired

of omnipotence, Peewee offers to play
for the CEO-ship of the cosmos, then designs
to triple bogey the first five holes.

After the game, when Fool's sworn in,
the meek finally do inherit the earth.
For a while, even gluttons and bullies

find themselves saying "May I?"
and "After you." Everyone's a guest,
sipping bubbly at a rose-tinted window,

till Peewee, who dearly misses his toadies
and hit lists, harangues those milquetoasts
into worshipping the ground he scurries over.

As the trumpet of doom dumps its sour note
into the milk and honey, the rich regain
their leverage, the poor re-queue for crusts.

It's back to square one, almost, with God
in his ShoeLifts and Fool unright with the world,
this time down to the remotest lepton,

though nobody gives much weight
to God's pronouncements anymore,
he's so small, and his tinny voice such a pain.

DANCIN' FOOL

"Danse Fantastique," he calls it, a light elixir
for lousy days, nice ones, too. Frankly,
he's not sure one time's better than another:
He's no expert. This is not a dance for experts,
just the opposite, so he doesn't have to get
what you'd call "good" at it; he doesn't have to
make a spectacle of himself like the Rockettes
or the Thrones, Dominions, or Principalities. This
is for fools who don't dance, who can't swing
their arms with their torsos, who are always
asking themselves "*Whose* left, mine or yours?"
or "What *is* the right moment?"—fools who think
they'd look like some kind of Saint Vitus if they tried
to learn the Tango or the Marenge, who've learned
to keep their feet square and their chin protected.
Never mind the fancy name: it's just to make the thing
sound classy, continental. It's for the media. He starts
this dance easy, no gyrating or high kicks;
just works slowly through the positions, which
it helps him to think of as on those big cards
with the footprints, the Arthur Murray method.
He practices till he can do them in a row without
saying "Excuse me" till he almost turns blue,
without wondering where all the time went,
without the slightest blink—till he can do them
even when the trees look like hit men and he hears
the devil's stretch limo idling in his driveway,
and to some kind of music. Sometimes he just hums
something—"Singing in the Rain" for instance,

or even the theme from *Dirty Dancing*, if he
can remember it—as long as it's not syncopated
or march time. He doesn't have to learn
to use his arms and legs all over again like he
was turning into some kind of bird. Tell the truth,
it's just fooling around: there aren't any
positions as such; it's just a way of saying, "Better
now than when my ass falls completely off,"
of thinking of himself as Moon equipped, a low rider,
or, better yet, of not thinking at all, except
with his feet, those Mozarts, those Rachmaninovs.
It's more like walking, only with a little shuffle step
—like Dorothy and her sidekicks hoofing off to Oz—
a step he can change a little, or even leave out. Hey:
"Danse *Fantastique*," right? Nobody's holding up
scorecards. But, believe me, in six weeks
or less, somewhere along his figure-eight path
from Heaven to Hell and back, he knows
he'll be walking like Astaire, like Saint Bo Jangles,
and all about him there'll be wings, wings, wings.

Roll Out the Fool

*St. Chrysostom formulated the most
comprehensive and fundamental definition
when he described the Fool as "he
who gets slapped."*
   —Enid Welsford,
      The Fool: His Social and Literary History

In cave days, Fool mated
with the pratfall,
the hot foot, the bully's
brunt—his deadpan
so endearing when his head

met stone, he was voted
Best Victim.
The teens loved it.
Grownups, too.
He tamed their blood

pressure and kept
their world-view cheerful
as a cannibal ho-down.
But they wanted more,
something *real*

good: no more chipped
bicuspids or routine
flesh wounds.
So they'd make him
a clubbing dummy,

spear catcher, all day
torch, sabertooth lure.
Forest gatherings
lacked the proper tang
without a Flaming Fool,

Exploding Fool,
or—big mistake—
a Fool Frappé, which,
one snowy night,
everybody ate

like it was brain
food or something,
so now we've got
Fool in our marrow,
which explains

history, for one thing.

FOOLPROOF

"Just turn it *on*, *when* I tell you to," says God,
   ready to have the bubonic plague sucked up
   and shot into the Crab Nebula before it can harm a single
   14th-Century soul. "Any fool can do it," He snaps,
   as Fool fumbles at the controls of a galactic Hoover
   brought forth for the occasion. "Like this?" says Fool.

"Moron!" God thunders, watching a snot-green cloud
   pour out of His perfect wand for hard-to-reach places.
"They're going to crucify Me in the broadsides." Could be worse,
   thinks Fool, backdraft whistling through his hands and feet.

FOOL'S WAGER

Put your money on Fool and you win
a pair of his too-tight shoes, plus
death, taxes, and a front-row pass
to an old Stones concert, the one
where the Angels played Yankee Doodle
with pool cues on a xylophone
of numskulls and stabbed a guy
during "Sympathy with the Devil."

Your choice is Slough Two or Fen One,
unless you're toting a full pardon.
Get the picture? Here's a hint: Don't
make any sudden moves, and watch
for tripwires. Actually that was
two hints, which may not be enough
when you're hobbling the thousand-miles
that begins that doozie of a first step.

Biographical Note

A native Midwesterner, William Trowbridge was born in Chicago and grew up in Omaha. He holds a B.A. in Philosophy and an M. A. in English from the University of Missouri-Columbia and a Ph.D. in English from Vanderbilt University. His poetry publications include five full collections: *Ship of Fool* (Red Hen Press, 2011), *The Complete Book of Kong* (Southeast Missouri State University Press, 2003), *Flickers*, *O Paradise*, and *Enter Dark Stranger* (University of Arkansas Press, 2000, 1995, 1989), and three chapbooks, *The Packing House Cantata* (Camber Press, 2006), *The Four Seasons* (Red Dragonfly Press, 2001), and *The Book of Kong* (Iowa State University Press, l986). His poems have appeared in more than 30 anthologies and textbooks, as well as in such periodicals as *Poetry*, *The Gettysburg Review*, *Crazyhorse*, *The Georgia Review*, *Boulevard*, *The Southern Review*, *Columbia*, *Colorado Review*, *The Iowa Review*, *Prairie Schooner*, *Epoch*, and *New Letters*. He has given readings and workshops at schools, colleges, bookstores, and literary conferences throughout the United States. His awards include an Academy of American Poets Prize, a Bread Loaf Writers' Conference scholarship, a Camber Press Poetry Chapbook Award, and fellowships from The MacDowell Colony, Ragdale, Yaddo, and The Anderson Center. He is Distinguished University Professor Emeritus at Northwest Missouri State University, where he was an editor of *The Laurel Review*/GreenTower Press from 1986 to 2004. Now living in Lee's Summit, MO, he teaches in the University of Nebraska MFA in Writing Program. His hobbies include motorcycling on his Triumph Sprint 995 S/T, travel, and trying to keep the damn rabbits away from the hibiscus.